FREIGHT TRAINS

by Nikki Bruno Clapper

Consulting Editor: Gail Saunders-Smith, PhD

Consultant: Martin Wachs, PhD,
Distinguished Professor Emeritus
of Urban Planning, UCLA

Pebble® Plus

CAPSTONE PRESS
a capstone imprint

Pebble Plus is published by Capstone Press,
1710 Roe Crest Drive, North Mankato, Minnesota 56003
www.capstonepub.com

Library of Congress Cataloging-in-Publication Data
Cataloging-in-publication data is on file with the Library of Congress.
ISBN 978-1-4914-6038-2 (library binding)
ISBN 978-1-4914-6058-0 (eBook PDF)

Editorial Credits
Nikki Bruno Clapper and Linda Staniford, editors; Juliette Peters, designer;
Jo Miller, media researcher; Kathy McColley, production specialist

Photo Credits
Dreamstime: Dmitriy Sladkov, 19 (top); Getty Images: Mike Danneman, 9; Newscom/Xinhua News Agency/Lu Jingli, 17, Shutterstock: Alexander Tihonov, 9 (inset), Darren Hedges, 7, Evlakhov Valeriy, 15, Gerard Koudenburg, 19 (bottom), Gritsana P, 2-3, 22-23, kraphix, cover (ticket), Maria Dryfhout, 21, Mayskyphoto, 1, Prasit Rodphan, 13, remik44992, 11, Serjio74, cover (train), Steve Design, 5, tovovan, train design element (throughout)

Note to Parents and Teachers

The All Aboard! set explores and supports the standard "Science, Technology, and Society," as required by the National Council for Social Studies. This book describes and illustrates freight trains. The images support early readers in understanding the text. The repetition of words and phrases helps early readers learn new words. This book also introduces early readers to subject-specific vocabulary words, which are defined in the Glossary section. Early readers may need assistance to read some words and to use the Table of Contents, Glossary, Read More, Internet Sites, and Index sections of the book.

Printed in the United States of America in North Mankato, Minnesota.
022016   009561R

Table of Contents

At the Crossing

A horn blasts.

Red lights flash.

A striped gate comes down.

Car after car rumbles by.

The freight train has come!

Heavy Haulers

Freight trains carry coal, lumber, and other heavy cargo over long distances. One freight train hauls more than many trucks can.

At the front of a train
are diesel locomotives,
or engines. A few engines
can pull hundreds of cars.

Couplers keep cars together.

coupler

Freight trains can be

3 miles (5 kilometers) long.

On open track they often

travel about 50 miles

(80 km) per hour.

Types of Freight Cars

The flatcar is the oldest type of freight car. It has no sides and no roof. Today's flatcars carry huge containers filled with products.

A gondola is an open car
with sides. It carries loose
cargo such as sand or gravel.
One gondola holds 100 tons
(90 metric tons) of freight.

A boxcar keeps cargo dry.
It has sides and a roof.
A boxcar can carry just
about anything, from paper
to machines.

Hoppers have chutes for
unloading coal or grain.
Tank cars hold liquids like oil.
Refrigerator cars keep meat,
milk, and vegetables cool.

hopper car

chutes

tank car

Spotlight:
The Caboose

Some train workers used to
do their work in a caboose.
In the 1980s computers
took over this work. Trains
no longer need cabooses.

GLOSSARY

car—one of the wheeled vehicles that are put together to form a train

cargo—objects carried by a train, ship, aircraft, or other vehicle

chute—a narrow slide; coal pours out of hoppers on chutes

coal—a black or dark brown rock that can burn

coupler—a device at either end of a railroad car that links it to other cars

diesel—a heavy fuel that burns to make power

freight—goods that are shipped from one place to another

haul—to pull or carry a load

liquid—a wet substance that can be poured

locomotive—the railroad car that holds the engine to pull the train

lumber—boards cut from logs

READ MORE

Goodman, Susan E. *Trains!* Step into Reading. New York: Random House, 2012.

Klein, Adria F. *City Train.* Stone Arch Readers. North Mankato, Minn.: Stone Arch Books, 2013.

Peters, Elisa. *Let's Ride the Subway!* Public Transportation. New York: PowerKids Press, 2015.

INTERNET SITES

FactHound offers a safe, fun way to find Internet sites related to this book. All of the sites on FactHound have been researched by our staff.

Here's all you do:

Visit *www.facthound.com*

Type in this code: 9781491460382

Check out projects, games and lots more at
www.capstonekids.com

INDEX

Word Count: 205

Grade: 1

Early-Intervention Level: 18